LEADERSHIP WRECKS
How Poor Leadership Impact Organizations and People

Dr. Christine Fuselier
©2018

ISBN: 9781096241317

Copyright ©2018 Christine Fuselier. All rights reserved, this book, or parts thereof, may not be reproduced in any form without written permissions from the author; exceptions made for brief excerpts used in published reviews

Published By

CreateSpace Independent Publishing Platform, North Charleston, SC

There was a time when Leadership stood for Integrity, Class and Respect. Over the past few years, there has been a Leadership shift for the worse, and it is destroying our organizations and the people who work in them.

-Dr. Christine Fuselier

Speak Truth to Power
-Anonymous

PREFACE

Over the past decade or so there has been a leadership education explosion. There are countless books, seminars, workshops, Ted Talks, conferences, and so much more on the topic of the leadership phenomenon that has taken us by storm. With all the leadership resources available one may wonder, why is there still such poor leadership in our communities, churches. political stages, homes, and organizations.

Leadership is often underrepresented in action and overrepresented in titles. Leadership Wrecks is about the pitfalls of those in leadership positions and the negative impact they have on the people and organizations they lead. As organizations suffer from growing leadership gaps, there needs to be a way to identify why the gaps occur, ways to bridge them and strategic preventative measure to minimize them from reoccurring. This book will provide real-life scenarios, the impact of the scenarios, and analysis on ways to rethink the scenarios.

To fully understand the impact; good, bad, or ugly leadership has, we first must know what it is. There are countless leadership gurus with countless definitions or interpretations of leadership. I thought it would be interesting to break down the word leadership in the most basic form: LEAD - be in charge or command + ER - denoting a person, animal, or thing that performs a specified action or activity + SHIP - a large boat used for traveling long distances over the sea. From these operational definitions, one can deduce that leadership is the action of an individual in command over large specific activities, people or places with far reaching and lasting impacts. Leadership transcends across various situation, industries, span of control and locations.

This book is about several damaging leadership styles, experiences and impacts that are often overlooked, underestimated, and over celebrated. As organizations struggle through what many see as a leadership crisis, this exploration will provide insight on how these recent brands of leadership have re-emerged and are being accepted, promoted and celebrated.

TABLE OF CONTENTS

Preface……………………………………………....5

Divisive Leadership……………………………..11

Bully Leadership….....………………………….22

Reactive Leadership……………………...………33

Ivory Tower Leadership………....………………41

Profit Driven Leadership…………………......……50

Blind-Eye Leadership-……………………… ….59

Immoral Leadership ….... …………………….…..67

Egotistical Leadership……...…………………….74

Emotional Leadership……….…………………...81

Transactional Leadership…….....……………...89

Petty Leadership…………………………………97

Poser Leadership……...…………….……………104

Checkbox Leadership…………………………….111

Nepotistic Leadership……………………………117

Workplace PTSD………………………………….125

Conclusion..127

References..129

About the Author....................................133

DIVISIVE LEADERSHIP

There is more power in unity than division
- Emanuel Cleaver

Divisive leadership is a way of segregating individuals and departments to promote unhealthy competition and alliances in office politics. While many organizations may need to have divisional structures to compartmentalized departments, they do not have to divide the people to create a culture that is not unified. If you run your organization or department by dividing people, you will never be able to lead them, and they will ultimately not respect you. It's impossible to lead people who do not respect you. Divisive leadership is shown by those with low self-esteem and low self-worth, and by dividing their team, they feel a sense of power.

A leader who promotes divisiveness does not really care about the organization's success but has a personal agenda to maintain his or her sense of control and dominance. A divisive leader tells his or her directs to only take guidance or direction from them. He or she exhibit behavior of anxiousness when they see two or more of their direct reports talking, congregating, or collaborating. Divisive leaders do not promote collaboration, nor do they encourage teamwork; further they are uneasy when they see teammates bonding for fear of them comparing notes and discovering the leader's true motives and see the leaders' incompetence.

A sign of a divisive leader is to tell directs not to talk to other teammates. As juvenile as it sounds, they want to horde influence to keep an individual on their side. It may be disguised by saying, "I don't want you to be burned by associating with them" or "I have big plans for you" or "it's not good to have friends at work" or "I don't want you taking advice from anyone but me." This type of culture creates dissention and distrust which a divisive leader thrives on. Why? Because if you foster an environment where there is little interaction or collaboration, the chances of people working together, learning from one another, growing together comparing notes are minimal which makes a divisive leader feel in control.

Real-Life Scenario:

A Director spoke to employee individually to tell them not to take advice, and limit talking to anyone else within the department or organizations about rules, policies, or complaints. He did not promote collaboration amongst the team, instead he threatened the team members career growth if they do not do as they are told or follow his lead. The Director further befriended certain team members to gain their confidence and learns personal information to use against them later. He used the information learned to tarnish an individual's reputation. He would also have sidebar meetings and give team members conflicting directives to create contention for the purpose of promoting divisiveness. He hired a new young employee and informed her in order to grow in the company she must only talk to him, get direction from him, and not share any ideas she has with anyone but him. Being a young, eager manager, she felt that was the way to lead.

Impact to the Organization:

This type of behavior created distrust of leadership and divisiveness in the workplace. There is no comradery among the team and the behavior is imbedded in the culture. Morale is low, production is low, and turnover is high which causes both reputational and financial damage. Divisive leadership fosters a 'crabs in the barrel' or 'don't go against the grain' culture. A prime example of this is: after the 2016 presidential election, GrubHub CEO, Matt Maloney sent a strong anti-Trump email to all employees: "I absolutely reject the nationalist, anti-immigrant and hateful politics of Donald Trump," he wrote. "If you do not agree with this statement then please reply to this email with your resignation because you have no place here." This resulted in a social media boycott and dramatic drop in their stock Matt Maloney later tried to clarify, saying he didn't mean that anyone who voted for Trump should quit, but the damage was done (Maloney, 2016). This is not only divisive, its stifling, and anti-diversity. While divisive leadership in not new in organizations, as of late, there seems to be a license to openly divide teams, groups, and departments. With weak leadership this type of divisiveness is ignored, overlooked and never addressed. Weak leaders are either intimidated by the person spearheading the divisiveness (if it's not them) or agree with the behavior. Either way, as it's been proven time and time again, divisive behavior does not turn out well for the organization in the long run.

Do you agree with this behavior? If so why? Why not?

As a leader, what would you do differently? Why

Message from The Doctor:

Lincoln said it best "A house divided against itself cannot stand." This not only applies to our homes, it applies to organizations, politics, churches, and relationships. If you promote an environment of division, you show how much you don't care about the success of the organization. Division is a symptom of selfishness, which is a sign of weakness. To get over the selfishness that causes leadership to promote divisiveness one first must admit it, then start to build self-confidence and self-love. Just because you're in a leadership role doesn't mean you have confidence and typically it shows up in petty behavior such as divisive leadership.

Building self-confidence will require you to increase your knowledge about yourself (ex. self-reflections, read a book, conferences). Build on your strengths. Do a self S.W.O.T analysis (Strength. Weakness. Opportunities. Threats). This type of self-analysis allows you to study your mistakes. After you have identified your opportunities and weaknesses you then have a blueprint to help develop new skills.

Working on improving yourself takes time and is continual. If you've identified with the divisive leadership style, your first step is to stop the division within yourself. Create tactical strategies to improve your divisive behavior. Hold yourself accountable or get someone who will. As with any strategy, its only as good as its executed.

BULLY LEADERSHIP

I realized that bullying never has to do with you. It's the bully who's insecure. -Shay Mitchell

As in the playground, a bully is a person who thinks he/she have the upper hand because of his/her size or strength. Workplace bullies who engage in these behaviors are males 60% of the time. While men who bully tend to victimize both genders equally, women bullies target other women about 80% of the time. We see bullying in the workplace because of one's position, title, or tenure in an organization. In true bully form, a bully leadership style rules by creating an atmosphere of intimidation, inadequacy, fear, or anger. Bully leaders are not able to take on someone who is fearless and equally or more competent than they are. They go after the people with less experience, time with the organization, or not as confrontational. They are very threatened by people who stand in their own power, call them out on their nonsense and hold them to a higher standard.

Bully leaders can disguise themselves as being protective when they are destructive. Just like in most cases of bullying, leadership allows the behavior, often gives permission by forewarning the recipient of the bullying that it just "a tough leadership style".

Signs of bully leadership are: criticizing a subordinate's work in front of others, typically it is petty and insignificant criticism not given to help but to hurt; defaming one's reputation with blatant lies or twisted the truth by trying to make one seem inadequate; making threats directly or indirectly, typically the latter because a bully has no backbone or courage to speak truth. Putting a bully in a leadership position gives them the authority to push people around and break the rules. Bully leadership is often disguised as micromanaging (which by the way, if your micromanaging, it a true sign that you cannot manage) and setting expectations or goals that cannot or never have met. Bully leaders use phrases like "if you don't do it you will be out of a job" or " No one will do or say anything to me because I know where the bodies are buried" or " you're only equal to me on paper" or " you need to bull through your team to make them do what you want them to do." A bullying leader is one who is extremely insecure and display no emotional intelligence because he/she is impulsive based on how they feel.

Real-Life Scenario:

As a new leader was seeking advice of how to lead a team she inherited which was a bit challenging for her, her boss who had been in a leadership role for many years proceeded to explain to her that "sometimes you must treat your subordinates like dogs, grab them in the collar and step on their necks until they submit, this is how you establish your power and dominance." She further shared that people are dispensable and if they did not conform, they are replaceable. She explained to this new leader, how her goal was to make things uncomfortable for certain people to force them to quit. This individual also used the phrase "do as I say, not as I do." While these instances were sad, it was even sadder to see the wide-eyed new aspiring leader soaking in this advice like a sponge and began to change her approach based on what was learned from the bullying boss. As suspected, she emulated the behavior and the speak of her boss, which resulted in a high turnover rate, poor moral, and a decline in quality customer service.

Impact to the organization

Bullying behavior in organizations impacts what future leaders think leadership looks like. It will create an upcoming generation of bullying leaders, which in-turn creates organizations that become the worst places to work. The bully's pulpit encompasses abusive tactics that shows lack of respect, make employees feel uncomfortable, inadequate, sad or angry, which will ultimately lead to a hostile work environment. Thinking about the root of where bullying comes, whether it happens on the playgrounds, social media, boardrooms, political offices, or churches, it stems from the bully being uncomfortable, inadequate, sad or angry. If there is no accountability for bullying leadership, the organization will fail, or the cycle will continue. Bully Leadership is the biggest cause of workplace PTSD. Individuals who leave organizations that foster bullying have difficulty recovering from how it made them feel and some never recover.

Do you agree with this behavior? If so why? Why not?

As a leader, what would you do?

Why?

Message from The Doctor:

Bullying is a learned behavior. You must see a bully to be a bully and that behavior is seen at home (by a parent or spouse) and shows up in the workplace. Being a bully in a leadership role simply magnifies the bully behavior. A leader bullies because they feel powerless, forgotten and lack empathy, they have no ability to use more productive strategies to establish their power and presence. Bullying behavior show up in three fundamental ways, direct bullying, passive-aggressive bullying, and micro-aggressive bullying. Direct bullying is belittling, berating, or intimidating one on a regular basis, so much so it becomes normal behavior or the workplace culture. Passive aggressive bullying is not as direct and is harder to detect and is often expressed in subtle insults, sullen behavior, stubbornness or deliberate insubordination. Micro-aggressive bullying is probably the most dangerous, because the intended target may not see it coming. Often micro-aggressive bully shows up in the words used or not used, off handed comments, disguised as helpful or supportive but underhandedly sabotages other's success out of fear of being outshined.

If you identify with the characteristics of a bully, more than likely you are one and must know the impact the behavior has on the people you bully or the people watching you bully. Admission is the first step to recovery. Once you own the bully label, then you change it by first understanding what drives you to behave that way. As previously mentioned, bullying is a learned behavior and requires some analysis where it was learned from. Just like anything we learn, it can be unlearned, but we must put in the work.

REACTIVE LEADERSHIP

Reactive people are often affected by their physical environment. They find external sources to blame for their behavior. - Stephen Covey

Reactive leadership is when there is responsiveness after an incident or situation has occurred. Reactive leaders do not plan, forecast, or act proactively because they are not big-picture thinkers. They are not forward thinkers and have no leadership skills. A reactive leader is not good in a crisis and deflects his/her incompetence and inconsistencies on others. They are typically out of control, irrational or play the blame game in times of crisis. There is no root cause, research or preventative measure with reactive leaders because they are either operating in the moment or waiting for something to happen. They are so reactive, they do not take time to reflect to see how they could have done better, but to justify their reaction or prove how right they are in a situation. A reactive leader does not delegate, promote teamwork, advocate a trusting environment or mentor others. However, they are quick to blame and degrade others when something goes off the rails.

Real-Life Like Scenario:

A Manager fires a lead technician because a process the manager was responsible failed which caused a huge financial loss to the organization. While the manager was responsible for the process, he did not plan, delegate or collaborate with the technician to ensure all things were in place to make sure the process would work. Instead of the manager admitting he did not proactively plan, he blamed and fired technician and continued to destroy his reputation. Some things that were later found out was the technician had very little authority, was not empowered and when he asked questions or raised concerns he was ignored. Even after the failure occurred, the manager never thought to put preventative measures in place to avoid the incident from occurring in the future.

Impact to the Organization:

Reactive leadership has reputational, cultural, and financial damage. In this real-life scenario, the organization lost a technician who added intellectual value, knew and created many of the processes. The organization's morale was impacted because employees who saw it happen felt they were not valued and or would be targeted next. The financial impact to the organization came from being sued for wrongful termination. Reactive leaders have no proactive or forward-thinking abilities. There was no thought leadership being demonstrated, taught or encourage which impact the growth of the organization. Because there were no preventative measures put in place, similar incidents occurred and continued to cost the organization money.

NOTES

Do you agree with the behavior? If so why? Why not?

As a leader, what would you do?

Message from The Doctor:

A reactive leader is simply responsive. They do not have the ability to be proactive or to plan. This could be caused by a leader never learning or never being taught the value of planning or forward thinking. While there are situations when being reactive is warranted because there are unforeseen circumstances, it should not be normalized by leadership. When a leader is always in reactive mode, it is a symptom that there is a lack of vision, foresight, taking initiative, or sound decision-making abilities. Often reactive leaders are just waiting for something to happen before they do anything, or they regurgitate what they see. To change this style requires a shift in one's mindset and critical thinking about how to move the organization forward in a way that motivate and inspires others to do the same. Employing forward thinking strategies, will minimize how much one needs to be in reactive mode.

IVORY TOWER LEADERSHIP

Policies that emanate from ivory towers often have an adverse impact on the people out in the field who are fighting the wars or bringing in the revenues. -Colin Powell

Ivory Tower Leadership is leadership that is extremely disconnected from their organization. They have no clue what happens on the front line. The ivory tower leader is known to stand up in a town hall meetings and tout about the organization's culture which is typically off base because they spend no time in the trenches or with the people doing the work. They are simply out of touch. Some may argue that it's because they are working on big picture strategic initiatives and they expect their direct reports to be in touch with the people. The perception of the people doing the work on the frontline is that Ivory Tower leaders do not relate to them nor do they care about them. Ivory Tower leadership can form one's decision making through sound bites from a select few people (typically their leadership team) without seeing or being aware of other agendas (but in some cases they are very much aware). Ivory Tower Leaders are not courageous enough to have skip-level meetings (which are one on one meetings with your leadership team's direct reports) because they have built buffer with their "yes men (or women)," they cannot separate themselves from their own importance. This looks to others in the organization like they do not have the time or don't care what's going on in the trenches. Ivory Tower Leaders are always up for a photo op. "The Ivory Tower Leader can become out of touch with the experiences and problems of those that actually get the work done. Often the people at the bottom of the organizational hierarchy who make and design products and services, or who interact directly with the customers rarely could interact with Ivory Tower Leaders, due to no fault of their own. (Leaderstoday.org).

Real-Life Scenario:

During a town hall meeting a CEO was giving his yearly presentation about the health of the organization. This CEO was rarely seen by the general population of the various sites that he led throughout the USA. As he reviewed the financial status, upcoming initiatives and discussed the members of his leadership team, it sounded like he was talking about a different organization. During the questions and answer period, an employee asked, specific questions about their location, another asked, how often did the CEO visit the office throughout the USA?" The CEO looked stunned, embarrassed, and quite irate. He never made any adjustment to meet his employees where they were. A few people were terminated for asking question in a public forum and some for agreeing with those who spoke out.

Impact to the Organization:

While many agreed about the financial health and the new initiatives of the organization, they were in disbelief about how the CEO talked about the care they have for their employees. Many employees felt ignored and devalued by their leadership. Employees felt leadership was out of touch and during the town hall those feelings were confirmed. There was degradation of the reputation of the organization being a good place to work. While it may be a stretch (for some) to expect senior leaderships to get in the trenches, connect with the employees and understand the talent they have within their organization, those are the very things that can make or break an organizations success. . Ivory-Tower Leadership fosters an environment that leadership doesn't care about the people they are charged to lead. This behavior makes employees feel disconnected and they in turn disconnect.

*******NOTES*******

Do you agree with the Director's behavior? If so why?

Whynot?_____

As a leader, what would you do? Why?

Message from The Doctor:

Ivory Tower Leaders are not in touch with the people they lead because they do not take the time to connect or can no relate to their team members. In some cases, it's by design, in others it's by defect. A symptom of Ivory Tower Leadership is dare not getting in the trenches with your team. They never see you do what you expect them to do. Sometimes they have never seen you except at a town hall or the organization's website. Ways to improve this behavior is come down from the tower occasionally. Have lunch with employees, eat in the cafeteria where your employees eat (you'd be surprised at what you learn). Stop treating them like your employees and treat them like your partners. Respect the work that they do and the skillset that they have and show them by valuing what they bring to the table. Don't be afraid to come down from the Ivory Tower and get in the trenches.

Profit Driven Leadership

A business that makes nothing, but money is a poor business -Henry Ford

Profit driven leadership is all about the dollars. They strictly run the business by the numbers. The focus is not about what is best for the customer or employee. While all companies are in business to make money, leading for money can cause a leader to lose their integrity and stop others from respecting them. They do things that are immoral, unethical, and often illegal to turn a profit which typically backfires; works for the short term or there is always a deficit or the need to continually chasing the money. You can't benefit from doing the wrong things even if it is for the right reasons. A good leader knows how to turn a profit without turning stomachs. Profit driven leaders underpay their employees and line their pockets opposed to re-investing into development of their people and the communities they serve. More times than not

Profit Driven Leaders treat the organizations money like their own personal piggy bank.

****NOTES****

Real-Life Scenario:

An employee had to have a life impacting, time sensitive surgery and pre-scheduled it. Because of the culture in the organization and the focus on profit, it was indirectly suggested that the employee move the surgery back a week or two to help their team get more customers to book more loans. Because of the cultural pressures, the employee moves his surgery date. A member of the leadership team continually touted how loyal the employee was for basically putting his health at risk to help the company book more loans, which could have (or should have) been done by any other team member. The individual did get promoted as a result of his "dedication" & loyalty." This type behavior became the expectation in the organization and the running joke became "profit beats pride."

Impact to the Organization:

Many of the worker's peers and other members of management saw the request as disgusting for leadership to not only condone but praise the employee for what they deemed a grand gesture. This incident impacted how many of the employees saw their leadership, which was selfish, inconsiderate, with no regard for the workers' health and a poor example of loyalty to the organization all in the name of profit. Others expressed fear, no work life balance, believed showing loyalty meant putting your health or family at risk. Some workers saw it as the way to survive and get promoted. One worker fell down the stairs at home, hurt his head and ended up with a concussion, but dare not go to work because of the expectation that has been set. Leadership allowed him to come in and work for a few days, until his literally passed out and was forced to stay home, all the while thinking his job was in danger.

The leadership saw the bottom line (dollars) was way more important than making sure their employee was OK.

****NOTES****

Do you agree with the Director's behavior? If so why? Why not?

As a leader, what would you do? Why?

Message from The Doctor:

As a business it is understood that making a profit contributes to the success of the organization. The question is at what cost? It is not only dangerous, but careless to foster an environment where an employee feels they must risk his or her health to prove "loyalty" in the name of the bottom line. Symptoms of profit driven leadership are crossing or straddling the ethical line (lying, cheating, or stealing); putting someone's health in danger for the bottom line; showing or telling your employees how their jobs are only dependent only on growth and dollars; squandering the company's money for personal needs or interest. To get better in this space, revisit the organization's vision (very few are all about profit). Remember the purpose of your role, and while yes, a part of it is to position the organization for profit, it not all of it. Define what success is to you and what you want your legacy in the organization to be. Change the running joke from "profit beats pride" to a running theme "Principles over Profit."

****NOTES****

BLIND-EYE LEADERSHIP

Leading with a blind eye does injustice to your organization because what you refuse to see others see clearly,
- *Dr. Christine Fuselier*

Blind-eye leadership is having undesirable information or being aware of information that you chose to ignore or simply not act on. As a leader, this impacts your reputation and can bring down an organization. Because you chose to turn a blind eye, does not mean it did not happen or that others will turn a blind eye. There can be legal implications of turning a blind eye which is known as willful blindness. Willful blindness is a legal concept that started in the nineteenth century and refers to a situation in which an individual could have and should have known something, the law treats it as if he or she knew it. If there is bullying, unethical, illegal, discriminatory, sexist behavior happening in your organization; claiming ignorance won't cut it. Watch the news and you will see how organizations and those who lead them are often destroyed by blind-eye leadership ranging from money laundering, employee discrimination to predatory lending. Typically, everyone around the leader sees the bullying, unethical behavior, discrimination, and sexism and they are expecting some type of accountability. In smaller organizations it is harder to call out because many of the team members "grow up together," meaning they have been working together all or most of their career and are part of the organizational culture. On the other hand, some of team members either don't want to see the poor leadership behavior, or have no idea of how to address, manage, or hold anyone accountable. In larger organizations, it is more intimidation because the repercussions can be career assassination.

Real-Life Scenario:

Turnover for a department was consistently at 80%. Several employees from the department informed the leadership team that the causes were blatant bullying, discriminatory, and unfair practices. The manager heading the department, lied, falsified documents, and coerced other employees to support lies. The department happened to be the highest profit center (cash cow) of the organization, therefore leadership turned a blind eye to the behavior, complaints, documentation provided all in the name of the bottom line. There was never any investigation of the complaints. Those who complained were either terminated, quit, or were moved to different departments.

Impact to the Organization:

Blind eye leadership causes reputational damage and legal standard can be called into question. Employees who witnessed this behavior unfold question the ethics and morals of the leadership team, that alone should be alarming. Author Margaret Heffernan describes "When the British Member of Parliament, Adrian Sanders, asked Rupert and James Murdoch if they were familiar with the term "willful blindness," their silence said it all. The MP defined it for them "If there is knowledge that you could have had, should have had but chose not to have, you are still responsible." Lack of such responsibility destroyed the departments reputation, manager heading the department lost credibility and respect from his peers.

Do you agree with the Director's behavior? If so why? Why not?

_____
_____
_____
_____
_____
_____
_____
_____
_____
_____
_____
_____
_____
_____

As a leader, what would you do? Why?

Message from The Doctor:

Blind-eye leadership is cowardly behavior. A coward is afraid to stand up against what is right or acknowledge what is wrong. It is easier for them to turn or walk away. Blind-eye leaders choose to ignore and then claim ignorance because to do otherwise forces him or her to take responsibility for the behavior they are turning a blind-eye to. That behavior is typically unethical, illegal, immoral, embarrassing or all the above. Typically, turning a blind eye for the sake of the "cash cow', ends up with the leader becoming the sacrificial lamb.

It is advised to be a standard bearer and establish integrity. The saying "if you see something, say something" holds true, but as a leader you have the power to also **_do something_** or step down and allow someone with the courage and integrity to step up.

****NOTES****

IMMORAL LEADERSHIP

The world is yearning for strong leadership and moral clarity; someone who knows the difference between good and bad. - Isaac Herzog

Immoral Leadership is having no moral compass and operating knowing what society considers right and wrong but do wrong anyway. An Immoral Leader guides and demonstrates immoral behavior like lying, cheating, stealing, and much worse. He or she can influence and persuade others in a negative, non-productive way. Immoral Leadership is centered around selfishness and unfairness. Immoral leadership denies the opportunities for others to cultivate and develop their leadership skills and abilities. Immoral Leadership values rank, power or position and lacks a deep sense of ethics, justice, equality, fairness, and the greater good. Immoral leaders have mastered self-centered leadership which caused them to be not only to be ineffective but untrustworthy as well.

Real-Life Scenario:

A leader takes costly, unnecessary business trips to tend to personal family issues or take family vacations. The same leader has employees run their personal errands on company time (picking up lunch, clothes from the cleaners). They once asked an employee to borrow money, then told them to put extra hours on their time sheet to get paid back. Every situation was justified by the leader constantly touting how much they did for the company and how much of their time and family time they gave to the company. They went on about how if it was not for them the company would not be in existence or make it through the tough times. They make comments like "that's why I get paid the big bucks" or "that's why I'm in charge," On the occasion they are confronted, they play the victim to gain sympathy.

Impact to the Organization:

Several employees left the organization and discouraged anyone from working there because when senior leadership was informed of the behavior, the immoral leader stayed in place. The employees did see a parade of senior leadership and human resources come down from corporate, interview employees, ask questions, penalize the employee who gave candid responses. Nothing happened to the leader.

There was a mass exodus from the organization. The leadership stayed in place, brought in new employees and the behavior continues. Regardless to the reputational and financial damage, the immoral thread and fiber in the company was sewn tighter than risking taking the moral high ground.

****NOTES****

Do you agree with the Leader's behavior? If so why? Whynot? _____

_____

_____

_____

_____

_____

_____

_____

_____

_____

_____

_____

_____

_____

As a leader, what would you do? Why?

Message from The Doctor:

Immoral Leadership is a disease that must be treated immediately before it spreads. If not dealt with, it becomes an epidemic within your organization. To treat it, you must first triage. Quickly identify the source of the immorality and get it out of your organization. If it goes untreated, it will spread until it kills the organization. If you do not know how to treat the disease of immoral leadership call in an expert.

EGOTISTICAL LEADERSHIP

Your ego can become an obstacle to your work. If you start believing in your greatness, it is the death of your creativity. -Marina Abramovic

Egotistical Leaders can be one of the most destructive kind of leader. They are excessively conceited, self-centered, *and* tend to have narcissistic personality disorder. While Narcissistic and egotistical behavior operate in the same vein one can be more destructive than the other in leadership roles. Egotistical leaders misuse company funds, resources, people, policies and procedures for their own self-gratification. They justify it in the name of the business when it really is about serving their own purpose. They tend to rest on their laurels or others backs with no innovation or initiatives of their own. They must be the center of their world and have a sense of importance by forgetting their role and position is for the betterment of the organization.

Real-Life Scenario:

During a staff meeting the team is charged with improving processes to become more efficient. As one of the team members outlines the various processes identified. Another team member identifies different methodology to prioritizes which process to select to work on first. The department leader has no input on processes identified or the methodologies presented but proceeds to take the next 25 minutes of the meeting to talk about how he pulled himself up by his bootstraps to make a career for himself and no one had ever climbed the corporate ladder like he had. As the team tried to refocus the leader on the topic at hand, he decided he would rather the team spend the next 30 minutes identifying what role did he play in their careers, explain the process of how it happened, and express the gratitude they had for him.

Impact to the Organization:

This was a waste of time, resources, money, and energy for the team members and the organization overall. This type of behavior was the norm for this department's leader, and again left the employees feeling helpless and worthless. While it never resulted in anyone leaving the organization, it caused the team members to become de-motivated and complacent which results in low morale. When you have demotivated, complacent team members they become disconnected from the organization vision and mission, and ultimately stunts its growth. An egotistical leader would not notice or care about the morale in his or her organization because nothing or no one is more important than them (or so they think).

Do you agree with the behavior? If so why? Why not?

As a leader, what would you do? Why?

Message from The Doctor:

A symptom of Ego Leadership is Ego Affliction. As with any afflictions, it causes pain and suffering specifically to those being exposed to it. It is curable providing you are willing to do the following: seek mentorship; have weekly listening sessions and be teachable which means you must be willing to learn. It is wise to have three mentors (who you trust, will tell you the truth and you are willing to listen to); one in your industries, one outside of your industry, and one who is the opposite sex/race than you. This will allow you to get a well-rounded perspective. Listening sessions will allow you to hear what is being said. The key to a listening session is you cannot talk. Finally, be open to learning which will require you to invest in your own self development. Learning can be done formally and informally. Through learning you will see the power of humility.

POOR EMOTIONAL-INTELLIGENCE LEADERSHIP

No authoritarian leader cedes power easily or turns it over to bodies he cannot control. -- Stephen Kinz

Poor emotional intelligence leadership is when leaders are more impulsive and act from an emotional-first perspective. A leader lacking emotional intelligence can get caught up making decisions based on feelings of jealousy, revenge, and frustration. Their decisions are more about how they feel verses facts or logic. A strong emotional leader has emotional intelligence and knows how to emotionally lead effectively, a quality not found in poor emotional leaders. Poor emotional intelligence leadership can lead to unethical decisions at times, because poor emotional leaders typically make decisions that protect themselves, their interest, opposed to decisions that include data, facts and inherently are ethical. Many of the emotions they display have lot to do with his or her own level of self-esteem. These types of leaders are overly emotional and unbalanced. In some cases, being emotional shows transparency, in other cases it shows one to be unstable, unpredictable or a loose cannon. Followers of emotional leaders get frustrated and confused by the inconsistency of emotions. This is typically when there is no emotional intelligence or self-control

Real-Life Scenario:

A supervisor who cannot tolerate anyone disagreeing with her, gets visibly upset whenever challenged even when there is merit to do so. One day the supervisor is questioned by someone in a meeting (who has more experience, credentials, education, and respect than her) and it sets off an emotional firestorm. The supervisor threw as full-blown tantrum and began inaccurately accusing and outright lying about the person who "had the audacity to question her." She then storms out of the room and slams the door. Thereafter, she launched a full-scale vendetta against the individual by lying, manipulating data to defame the individual's character, and singling the individual out with attacks and slanderous accusations. Meanwhile the individual's peers have said and done worse with not so much as a blink of an eye from said supervisor.

Impact to the Organization:

The behavior is so blatant the supervisor's peers, directs, and the whole department wonders why someone has not spoken out. The person who is targeted eventually leaves and has nothing good to say about the company. No one else feels comfortable asking questions, or having different opinions, or opposite thoughts from leadership simply out of fear for their jobs. Respect for the supervisors and her manager is lost and the department morale is at an all-time low. It appears to employees that upper management supports this supervisor's behavior, because it is not the first time and there is never any accountability or repercussions even when it was brought to upper management's attention.

Do you agree with the behavior? If so why? Why

As a leader, what would you do?

Why?

Message from The Doctor:

Daniel Goleman said it best "The most effective leaders are alike in one crucial way: They all have a high degree of what has come to be known as emotional intelligence." Emotional Intelligence is comprised of multipack of four and should be taken in large doses daily and they are: self-awareness, self-management, social awareness, and relationship management. Before you can effectively lead anyone else, you need to have self-awareness of your emotions and how you display them. If you have enough awareness of how your emotional intelligence, or lack thereof, have a negative impact to others you can then move to self-management. Self-management is about understanding your emotional triggers and how to adjust or eliminate them accordingly. Knowing your emotional trigger require a deep dive to learn yourself, measure your self-esteem, and understand your own self-worth. Once you learn how to self-manage, you can now better appreciate and leverage social awareness. Being aware of what's going on with others around you is how you gain their respect and willingness to be led by you. Showing people that you care about what is going on with them and the role and value they have within the organization is how you gain loyalty. To show social awareness you must have empathy, which is priceless. As you gain a handle on the top three (self-awareness, self-management, and social awareness) you should see significant improvements and can then take on relationship management. Relationship management is about duplicating your growth through coaching, development, and mentoring those you are leading or those looking to lead. Becoming an emotional intelligent leader allows you to be a transformational leader which will have a lasting impact.

TRANSACTIONAL LEADERSHIP

Transactional leaders tend to look at the world through a lens of punishment, rewards and or exchange for motivation. - Larry Ferlazzo

Transactional leadership is based on an exchange, transaction sometimes known as a quid quo pro. If you give good work or numbers you get rewarded, if you do not you get punished. If you don't tell the dirt that I have done, I will promote and protect you. There will be no training and development to help workers get better because that would mean giving up something first (it's easier to get rid of or demote someone verses teach and development them). That's the way of the world, right? A transactional leadership style survives best in a structured environment that has very limited exposure outside of the organization. The organizational culture is very cult like. According to transactional leadership theory, transactional leaders work within an organization's existing structure. It is difficult for them to think outside of the box, they are resistant to change but may say they want it. Transactional leaders are not relationship builders which is why it is difficult to maintain partnerships with other organizations or with "outsiders." They only network to get something from the people they meet. A transactional leader is great at pomp and circumstances, photo ops or sound bites, but are very hollow otherwise. They live by the mantra "if I can't get anything out of this for me, it's not worth my time," or "you scratch my back, I'll scratch yours."

Real-Life Scenario:

A Director has a team building session, she asks each member to describe a character that they are most like and why. As everyone goes around and shares, she's visibly surprised at what she heard. She then shares her character who she says is Lucy from Charlie Brown. She describes that she is most like Lucy, to put the football in front of her direct reports and when they go for the kick, she loves to snatch the ball and watch them fall. Her reasoning is, she doesn't get anything out of them kicking the ball successfully and her reward is to let them keep kicking and missing. She further explains that if she holds the ball and lets them kick it and they are successful, then they will get credit for kicking the ball, but she won't get credit for holding the ball. As far as she is concerned "if an employee does figure out how to kick the ball before she pulls it away, they are not worth investing, developing or coaching". She doesn't see the benefit of the ball being kicked, because she may not get the credit.

Impact to the Organization:

This changed the meaning of team building within the organization because it was the tone of most of the team meetings. In this situation many of the team members realized outside of being transactional, their leader was just mean spirited and could care less about them. As with most transactional leaders, the only value their employees have is what they can get out of them in that moment and time. This style can create a "crabs in a barrel" culture. Which means in their eyes an employee's failure somehow elevates their own success. Transactional leaders find a way of climbing over whomever he or she can to get to the top for the reward or recognition. Those who are not coached, trained, or mentored on how to move up are left at the bottom and devalued. When employees don't feel valued, they'll find organizations where they will be valued.

Do you agree with the behavior? If so why? Why not?

As a leader, what would you do? Why?

Message from The Doctor:

Transactional leadership has its place in some organizations. The key is understanding the side effects of poorly executed transactional leadership. In some cases, transactional leadership can promote abuse, silence and no tolerance for change. To be an effective transactional leader, you must practice open mindedness. Don't be afraid to do things differently, get out of the box and allow creativity. Be willing to be unapologetically disruptive to build relationship and connections with people and they will produce with and for you. Transactional Leadership should not be used to abuse your power, but to be empowering to others.

PETTINESS LEADERSHIP

"When you can't lead on a bigger scale, you focus on the smaller scale "– Unknown

Petty Leadership shows up when the one in the leadership role has insecurities or feels threatened by peers or subordinates. This leader struggles to provide recognition and rewards because they feel like your paycheck should suffice. Petty leaders marvel at highlighting minuscule failures. Petty leaders either have never had leadership training or don't understand how to apply any training they have had. They often can disguise themselves as micro-managers because they claim to see no issue as too small (which is not how that works). They display behavior that promotes negative cultures. Petty leaders focus on things that should be out of their purview because they don't know how to focus on the bigger issue, or they just want to flex their reach of power.

Real-Life Scenario:

A Project Manager leads and flawlessly implements an enterprise wide project that her organization has never done before. It brought more visibility to the organization and was a huge cost savings. The peers and other leaders of the Project Manager praised and recognized her for such a great job. The Director of the Project Manager called her in for what was thought to be recognition but turned out to be about how many 'post it' notes were used during the project planning. The director did not provide examples of how many 'post its' to use, or what was used in the past nor did she offer a recommendation of how many to use going forward. True to a petty leader's style this was a simple power play to indirectly reprimand a shining employee to dim her light all in the name of pettiness which is basically professional immaturity.

Impact to the Organization:

This behavior resulted in the loss of a yet another dedicated, strong employee who demonstrated her loyalty to the organization. This situation further discredited the Director's reputation of being a professional (internally as well and externally) because everyone saw her for how petty she was. Reputational damage was another impact, because as the word got on the street about the 'leadership style' people did not want to work for the organization. Finally, high turnover because this petty behavior was distasteful to other employees.

Do you agree with the behavior? If so why? Why not?

As a leader, what would you do? Why?

Message from The Doctor:

Pettiness leadership has less to do with who's being led and more to do with the leader. This is broken leadership because there are some internal inefficiencies that must be dealt with to rectify this behavior. Shifting your fixed mindset to a growth mindset allow you to see things at a higher level. As you start to focus on the higher level you have limited time to be petty. Also having controls in place when you feel the petty urges coming on. Ask yourself what value the pettiness will add, what impact will it have on the individual and organization and will it be worth the damage it will cause. If you still feel the petty urge, breathe, then turn it into a positive affirmation.

****NOTES****

POSER LEADERSHIP

"It isn't that they can't see the solution. It is that they can't see the problem." -G.K. Chesterton

Poser leaders just play the part. Their behavior shows up in two ways; they either don't say much or they are very scripted because they are afraid someone is going to find out what a fake leader they are. Alternatively, they say too much and overstate their abilities or experience because they are afraid someone will find them out. Either way they are secretly surprised they have the position they have. Somehow, they lucked out on a position and live in fear of someone challenging or calling them out for the posers they are, instead of putting effort to grow into their position. When someone who has more experience and truly does try to offer help or insight, the poser's defense is to discredit or try to silence them.

Real-Life Scenario:

A poser leader is promoted based on his ability to spin, politic and brag on how he knows where the bodies are buried. He hijacked meetings to reiterate something he did or an idea he stole many years prior. He could not express an original idea, thought or initiative of his own. When projects or events were being planned and worked on, this poser only showed up when the curtains open to take his bow and credit for the work his employees or peers have done. He continually misrepresents his abilities by talking the talk and not walking the walk.

Impact to the Organization:

Because most team members could see through the poser's façade, they had no respect for him as a leader or their boss. The only way they could stomach him was because of the position he held. The team demonstrated the practice of respecting the position not the person. Morale was low, turnover was high.

Do you agree with the behavior? If so why? Why not?

As a leader, what would you do? Why?

Message from The Doctor:

Just because you put lipstick on a pig, it's still a pig. No matter how well one dresses, loud they speak, or scripts they memorized, it does not cover up their inadequacies. Take off the mask. Being a poser is intellectually and physically exhausting. Believe it or not people see right through the mask. Oppose to be a poser, learn, train and get certifications (if applicable). Poser leadership shows up in defensive and attacking ways, simple because they do not want to be found out. The energy you put into posing can go toward developing and growing into a true leader.

****NOTES****

CHECKBOX LEADERSHIP

"Checkbox leader make a list and check it twice; they are insincere and cold as ice!" -Anonymous

Checkbox leaders just want to go through a list of things they can check off... sent an email check, gave instruction by passing someone in the hall, **Check!** Had a team meeting where they did 90% of the talking about nothing relevant to the meeting, **Check!** The checkbox leader is no deeper that the box they check. They don't realize they provide no substance or comprehend the impact their behavior has on others. In their mind, they are getting things done yet they do not correlate what they do with any value added to their team or organization. Checkbox Leaders call themselves a task master, but the only task they perform is checking the box. Typically, they don't have the mental ability to think beyond the box they check.

Real-Life Scenario:

A leader is tasked with training his staff for a new client they just signed which will double their business. The leader gives the staff a handout, then send the document to them in email. He then deems them trained. There is no explanation of the material, no training or scripts on alternative ways to deal with customer inquiries. When questioned about the inefficient training, the leader explains they have more important things to worry about than detailed training and if they gave them the material, they were trained (check!).

Impact to the Organization:

Just checking the box resulted in a poorly trained team, which resulted in misinformation provided to customers; frustrated employees; dissatisfied customers. Loss of customer and revenue. The checkbox mentality limits forward thinking, it also fosters missed opportunities for learning and growth. Checkbox leadership shows those aspiring to be leaders, that skill, and ability are not important or required to hold a leadership title.

Do you agree with the behavior? If so why? Why not?

As a leader, what would you do? Why?

Message from The Doctor:

Checkbox leadership is the bottom of leadership and merely indicates something was done; it does measure how well it was done. Check the Box Leaders are single functional and typically cannot make connections or build relationship. The have no thought leadership and no ability to think past the box they check. In some cases, the check the box mentality is effective but often this type of leader will never grow outside the box. Further what is the measure of success outside of checking the box.

NEPOTISTIC LEADERSHIP

Nepotism sometimes can be a lose-lose situation. -Vikram Chatwal

Nepotistic leaders hire, promote, and recommend people they are related to or have a relationship with. Hiring who you know or are familiar with in and of itself may not be so bad. The rub is when the person is not qualified or gets preferential treatment. Their bad behavior is overlooked (and sometimes rewarded) and they are not held accountable. Nepotistic leaders value their relationship over fairness, consistency and doing the right thing. While the nepotistic leader may think he or she is doing the friend or family member a favor, more than likely that are hurting them in the long run by being an enabler and not allowing them to thrive by earning the job or promotion. On the other hand, it can also be a way for the nepotistic leader to feed his or her ego by having someone indebted to them.

Real-Life Scenario

A leader hires their in-law for a senior position the individual had minimal experience in the industry and was not credentialed for the job. The leader forced the person on one of his department heads by always had 'sidebar' conversations about how the department should be ran, went to dinner and lunch with the in-law (for everyone to see). Because the in-law feels empowered, he comes in like a bull in a China shop, make rash and impulsive decisions, name drops to show his power, run up the company card, come and go as he please, and never does the assignments in a timely manner or at all. The behavior is rewarded with raises, promotions and extra time off.

Impact to the Organization:

This is one of the biggest morale killers. The team members observing the behavior are sometimes caught off guard and very insulted by what they witness. Typically, they leave when they realize nothing is going to change. If the company is not a "mom and pop" shop or run like one, the team members move elsewhere in the organization where the behavior is not tolerated or not so blatant. Often when individuals are hired because they are friends or family, they have a sense of entitlement, authority and power that typically goes unchecked. The victims of nepotistic leadership feel they have no recourse for fear of retaliation.

Do you agree with the behavior? If so why? Why not?

As a leader, what would you do? Why?

Message from The Doctor:

Nepotism only helps when the person is qualified and does not bring the sense of entitlement with them. While we all want to give our relatives a leg up, we must be aware of the impact nepotism has on fellow employees, moral, and your reputation. If that relative or friend is not qualified, committed or dedicated to doing the job, do them a favor and ***just say no***. Help them in other ways like coaching and developing them to improve their skills and introduce them to other people who can help set them up for success.

*****NOTES*****

WORKBOOK PTSD

"PTSD is a whole-body tragedy, an integral human event of enormous proportions with massive repercussions."
— Susan Pease Banitt

Posttraumatic stress disorder (PTSD) is often associated with military veterans. PTSD is also more broadly defined as when a person experiences something frightening, stressful or overwhelming. In the workplace one or all the poor leadership styles mentioned throughout this book can cause workplace PTSD at varying levels. Workplace PTSD is typically the result of a toxic work environment and can be developed when an employee underpaid, devalued or is the target or witness to bullying, reactive, immoral, egotistical, petty, divisive and nepotistic leadership. Workplace PTSD symptoms are not much different from those in people who experience other traumas. Some symptoms of Workplace PTSD may be nightmares, insomnia, trouble sleeping, feeling of dread, stress, anxiety, lack of pleasure in daily activities and angry outburst.

Often one does not realize they have workplace PTSD until they leave the toxic work environment. When they start working in an environment where they are valued, paid their worth, treated with dignity and respect, sometimes there's hesitation, fear and flashback of the place that caused the workplace PTSD. There needs to be an adjustment period, coaching and sometimes counseling for individuals working through his or her workplace PTSD.

Conclusion

Leadership is not a position; it is a purpose. We can lead from the top down to the bottom up, sideways and anywhere in between. As a society we seem to have lost the purpose of leadership. It's not about power, it'd about the ability to influence others in a positive, productive manner. We need to make leadership great again. As leaders, we must know that our words and actions matter and are positively impactful to those we lead. Those who are being led must hold leaders more accountable. There is too much at stake to allow those with their own agenda to be at the helm of our organizations, churches, and political offices. We must expect more and inspect what we expect by holding leaders accountable and not be afraid to speak truth to power and be unapologetic about doing so. Remember, leaders do what is allowed, permitted, and not challenged.

Being part of leadership does not mean you compromise your integrity by treating people unfairly, being inconsistent, unethical, or singling people out because of your insecurities. A true leader knows their worth and knows the value they can positively add to others. If you read this book and identified with some of the leadership described, consider ways to reinvent yourself to evolve and transform into a better leader.

References:

Baldoni, J (2018) How to deliver Moral Leadership to Employees Retrieved from https://www.forbes.com/sites/johnbaldoni/2018/04/12/how-to-deliver-moral-leadership-to-employees/#555193a037ba

Day, D. (2015) Reactive Leadership. The Leadership Circle Retrieved from https://leadershipcircle.com/reactive-leadership/

Gale, A. (2016) Why ego is toxic to leadership. Retrieved from https://www.managementtoday.co.uk/why-ego-toxic-leadership/leadership-lessons/article/1415069

Dryden-Edwards, R (N.D) Bullying retrieved from: https://www.medicinenet.com/bullying/article.htm

https://media.grubhub.com/media/press-releases/press-release-details/2016/Inclusion-and-Tolerance-in-the-Workplace/default.aspx

Llopis, G. (2017) 4 signs that Bosses Are Really Bullies

n.d. What is the Ivory Tower Syndrome in Leadership? Retrieved from http://leadertoday.org/faq/mistakeivory.htm

Neal M. Ashkanasy and Catherine S. Daus
The Academy of Management Executive (1993-2005) Vol. 16, No. 1, Theme: Focusing on the Positive and Avoiding the Negative (Feb. 2002), pp. 76-86
Schermerhorn, J.R., Hunt, J.G., & Osborn, R.N. (2005).

Organizational Behavior (9th ed.). New York: J

john Wiley & Sons, Inc.

Willful Blindness: Why We Ignore the Obvious at Our

Perils *Author:* Margaret Heffernan

ABOUT THE AUTHOR

Dr. Christine Fuselier AKA the Leadership Doctor

Whether leaders are born or made, they still must grow; Dr. Fuselier contributes to that growth by living is her destiny to cultivate transformational leaders Dr. Fuselier is a wife and a mother who tries to live as an example. Dr. Fuselier is a dynamic John Maxwell certified, speaker, trainer, coach and facilitator. She is a certified DISC trainer & consultant and a certified Myers Briggs consultant. Dr. Fuselier has been featured on 'CBS6-Virginia, This Morning', 1006.9FM Richmond Radio & various other Richmond radio stations', 1570am Chicago Radio', Chicago Defender newspaper', and Phoenix Magazine. Dr. Fuselier specialize in leadership growth & development utilizing a transformational learning model. This transformative empowerment model has been key to her success as a Higher Educator, Project & Program Manager, Operations Manager, Global Resourcing

Manager, Vice President, Senior Manager, Director, Business Owner and Author.

Dr. Fuselier previous publication was "The Business of You" a conversationally written book design to be a quick easy read that guides readers through a journey of self-leadership, self-assessment, self-accountability and self-love in preparation to evolve into one's destiny. It is available on Amazon.com, Barnes & Noble & Kindle.

www.ingramcontent.com/pod-product-compliance
Lightning Source LLC
Chambersburg PA
CBHW030014190526
45157CB00016B/2698